George Matheson

The Bible Definition of Religion

George Matheson

The Bible Definition of Religion

ISBN/EAN: 9783337100438

Printed in Europe, USA, Canada, Australia, Japan

Cover: Foto ©Lupo / pixelio.de

More available books at **www.hansebooks.com**

The Bible Definition of Religion ❧ ❧ ❧

BY THE

REV. GEORGE MATHESON, D. D.

"He hath shewed thee, O man, what is good; and what doth the Lord require of thee but to do justly, and to love mercy, and to walk humbly with thy God?" MICAH vi. 8.

NEW YORK   CHICAGO   TORONTO

Fleming H. Revell Company

Publishers of Evangelical Literature

Appreciation

By Marcus Dods, D. D.

Dr. Matheson's preaching is invariably profitable, full of suggestive and pregnant ideas, and enlivened by healthy optimism. This book is to all intents and purposes a sermon or sermons upon Micah's definition of religion, "to do justly, and to love mercy, and to walk humbly with God." Dr. Matheson urges that in order to do justly a man must put himself in his neighbor's place, must pass out of himself and incarnate himself in the life of his brother. "There can be no justice without sympathy, and there can be no sympathy without substitution," the substitution of myself for my fellow-man in his circumstances. Mercy in the Christian sense Dr. Matheson distinguishes from pity which is instinctive and painful; from the philosophical mercy which springs from the love of calm, deprecating hatred and revenge because they disturb self-culture; from the scientific mercy which is built upon the notion that man is a mechanism, and that to visit crime with penalty is a survival of the child's instinct to smash the door when he is angry. This scientific mercy is contemptuous. "The very ground of its forgiveness paralyzes its power to aid. It says, 'This is a helpless creature, and therefore not to be helped.' It pardons on account of incompetency; on account of incompetency it also passes by. It can refuse to *strike*, but it is nerveless to *redeem*." The mercy of Christ is founded on the opposite basis —the possibilities of man. "Walking humbly with God" receives in Dr. Matheson's hands a new interpretation. The humility in question is to be shown not toward God but toward man. A man is not to be proud of walking with God as a snob might be proud of walking with a duke ; but as he walks with God he is also to carry himself humbly toward his fellow-man.

Contents

The Bible Definition of Religion

Religion, says Christ, is love and love is gentle toward those with hollow eyes and famine-stricken faces * * * *And this religion of love takes on a thousand modern forms* * * * *For love is making the individual life beautiful, making the home beautiful, and will at last make the church and state beautiful* * * * *There is no force upon earth like divine love in the heart of man—and at last that force will sweeten and regenerate society.*—NEWELL DWIGHT HILLIS in " *Investment of Influence.*"

The

Bible Definition of Religion

"He hath showed thee, O man, what is good; and what doth the Lord require of thee, but to do justly, and to love mercy, and to walk humbly with thy God?" (Micah vi. 8.) Is that all? Are the relations between God and man of such a simple nature as this? Have men been tormenting themselves in vain? Have the sacrifices of all the ages been useless—of the Brahmin, of the Buddhist, of the Israelite himself? What shall we say of the *Christian*? Is this doctrine evangelical? You enter a church by the wayside. A young man mounts the pulpit, fresh from the university. He discourses on the obligation to pay your debts, on your duty to forgive injuries, on your need to realize that you are a poor frail mortal who have only a lease of life and must ere long give

up your place to another.   You have had a
sermon on the three virtues of Micah.   Do
you like it?   Not you.   You come out
with great dissatisfaction.   You say, "This
young man is one of the old Scottish Mod-
erates; I have not heard a word of the Gospel to-day; this is mere practical morality,
what might have been preached in the time
of Plato."   Yet this is Micah's creed; this
is the Bible's own definition of what religion is.   It cannot be explained as an ac-
commodation to Judaism, as a preliminary
training for benighted men.   The prophet
is not addressing a nation.   He says in so
many words that he is speaking to Man
—man universal, man cosmopolitan, man
wheresoever he may be found.   He is asking not what *we* need, but what God requires.   He is looking at religion not from
the side of earth, but from the side of
heaven.   He is asking, not "who is fit to
dwell in Jerusalem?" but "who is capable
of ascending into the hill of God, of dwell-

ing amid the blaze of His burning purity,
of subsisting unscathed in His eternal fire?"
In the light of the cross of Christ the answer
seems a startling one.

But let us look deeper, and I think we
shall come to a different conclusion. When
the question is asked, "Is this all?" I am
quite prepared to answer "Yes."   But I hold
that this "all," instead of being very little,
is in the moral sphere absolutely universal.
I think the error lies, not in the *creed* of
Micah, but in the belief that the practice of
that creed is a very easy thing. I main-
tain, on the other hand, that it is im-
possible it should be practiced with success
without a very advanced stage of the Christian principle. *Preached* in the time of
Plato it might be, but not *performed* in his
time, or at least not performed by his
method. Chronology has here no place.
We are not desirous to exclude from any
age the operation of the Christian principle.
But what we do say is that in no age of the

world could the creed of Micah be lived *without* the Christian principle. Neither the Scottish Moderate nor any other moderate is entitled to appropriate it. It demands, not moderation, but extremeness. It requires a state of mind the reverse of lukewarm. It needs the storm and stress of the spirit. It is no primitive condition of the religious mind. It is the ripest fruit of evangelical practice. It belongs rather to the finishing than to the authorship of our faith. The man who has mastered the Epistle of James has reached the summer of the soul.

"Do Justly"

Justice may be defined, that virtue which impels us to give every person what is his due. In this extended sense of the word it comprehends the practice of every virtue which reason prescribes, or society should expect. Our duty to our maker, to each other and to ourselves is fully answered if we give them what we owe them. Thus justice, properly speaking, is the only virtue, and all the rest have their origin in it.
—GOLDSMITH.

"Do Justly"

I PROPOSE to consider this in detail. I wish to take up briefly and separately each of these three requirements, and to show that it is not the *foundation*, but the final story, of the building. I begin with the first requirement, "Do justly." From the earliest times justice has been thought a most *prosaic* virtue. It was one of the four qualities which the Greek called the golden mean, to indicate the fact that it did not aim high. It was to him something intermediate between heights of heroic sacrifice and depths of human debasement —a sober landing-place which might be reached by all, and which involved no trouble in the climbing.

Now, I have no hesitation in saying that the Greek was wrong here—not in calling

justice a cardinal virtue, but in regarding it
as a golden mean. The truth is that this
so-called prosaic virtue of justice requires
those very heights of sacrifice from whose
elevation it is supposed to set us free.
When we read in the Epistle to the Gala-
tians that the law of Christ is "Bear ye one
another's burdens," our first impression is
that it is a step higher than common justice.
In truth, it is a step preliminary to it. There
is a familiar saying, "First just, then generous." As a matter of fact, it ought to
be reversed, "first generous, then just."
No man can be just until he has been generous. For consider what is implied in
justice. Nothing less than an emptying of
yourself into the life of another. The
reason why men are not just is their want
of sacrificial power. They fail to put themselves in the place of their brother man, to
look at him in their own mirror, to say,
"*Should* I like this done to *me?*" The
word "generous" literally means, "re-

membering the race." It suggests kindred sympathy, fellow-feeling, recognition of the fact that your neighbor has a nature like your own. It is the remembrance that he, too, laughs when he is happy and sighs when he is sad, is strong when he is fed and faints when he is hungry. And this is the preliminary to all justice—commercial, social, legal. I must become the substitute for my brother before I can be fair to him. I must take his nature, assume his circumstances, put myself in his place. I must give up myself in the meantime altogether, so far as I am distinct from him; I must live in his person, I must feel with his heart. Without this, I shall do him wrong.

Let me take a concrete example, and that from the simplest sphere—social life. One of your friends returns from town in the afternoon. You put a civil question to him; he answers with ill-natured quickness. You say to yourself, "Well, it

would be perfectly just that I should retaliate; but Christian principle restrains
me." You mean, of course, that it would
be right morally, but not evangelically.
But is it so ? *Is* it just that you should
retaliate ? Have you measured the circumstances ? Have you considered whether, in
the mind of your friend at that moment,
there was a sufficient amount of resisting
power to prevent him from being quick ?
Have you estimated the physical pain he
was suffering ? Have you measured the
weight on his mind ? Have you considered how he was fretted at the Exchange ?
Have you marked how little you yourself
were really the object of the explosion ? If
not, you are in no position to be just. This
so-called practical morality is in itself the
most *im*practicable of all things. It requires a previous act of sacrifice, a surrender of the soul. Thomas Carlyle cries for-
ever "do, do, do." But there is only one
state of mind that can begin by doing; it

is the state of the slave. The slave simply obeys; he knows the "what," but not the "why." But the freeman must begin with a thought—nay, with a transcendental thought. He must transcend himself, pass out of himself, incarnate himself in the life of his brother. To do a commonplace service he must yield up his own being, must lose himself, must live in another. The more commonplace the service, the more complete must be the surrender. Justice is a harder task than heroism, just because it is not heroic; and the man who is faithful in that which is least has required a deeper strain of sacrifice than he who is victor in that which is much.

It is a familiar doctrine of theologians that Christ "offered up a sacrifice to satisfy Divine justice"—to pay the debts of man. It is truer than some of these theologians dream of. It is not an abnormal, a miraculous thing. It is the illustration of a universal principle which holds always, every-

where. To estimate the debt of another is
not an easy thing; it demands a sacrifice.
It was a bold and a deep insight which
ventured to affirm that Christ Himself was
no exception to the law. To estimate the
debts of man He, too, had to descend—to
sacrifice. He, too, had to begin, not only
by self-forgetfulness, but by incorporating
a new self—a servant's form. He had to
put Himself in the place, in the environ-
ment of the debtor. He had to consider
His circumstances, to live within His ex-
perience. He had to measure the influence
of His heredity, the force of His passions,
the strength of His temptations, the con-
tagion of His surroundings, the power of
His examples, the bane of His upbringing.
All this and infinitely more, to Christ, to
you, to every living spirit, is involved in
estimating the moral debt of another.

What is your obligation to be just ? Is it
the civil and criminal courts of law ? The
large majority of unjust acts are not pun-

ishable by these courts. Is it the belief in a coming day of judgment? That is an obligation to self-interest, not to justice. Is it the welfare of the greatest number? In the order of nature number one is the greatest, and each man is for himself. Is it the existence of a power called conscience? That is the very thing to be explained. What *is* conscience? It means literally a "knowing together." In the things of this world it is the sight of my brother in my own looking-glass, my seeing of him in me. In the most common act of justice, I have, I must have, a double vision; he and I are reflected in one mirror. There can be no justice without sympathy, and there can be no sympathy without substitution. It is in vain that Moses gives the law until he has ordained the sacrifice. All the smoke of Sinai would not say to a man's heart "Thou shalt not steal," much less "Thou shalt not covet." The commandment must be created by another fire—a fire of inward sacrifice. The Gospel is older than the law, the only *possibility* for the law. Justice is the child of sympathy. The daughter looks homelier than the mother. Sympathy is the joy of the poet ; justice has been ever associated with life's prose. But it is in our poetic moments that our most prosaic duties are best performed, and it is through the gate of sacrificial love that we escape the mire of the common clay. We cannot rise from nature up to Christ. The Christian principle must be behind as well as before us—the Alpha as it is the Omega, the first as the last. The life of daily justice is lived by a breath of the life eternal.

"Love Mercy"

Two things this old world needs—tenderness and cheer. All about us are hearts hungry for sympathy, for kindness. We could do nothing better with our life than to consecrate it to a ministry of tenderness and encouragement. This is one of heaven's paths to happiness—for the merciful shall obtain mercy.—J. R. MILLER in "*Master's Blesseds.*"

" Love Mercy "

I COME now to the second article of the creed of Micah—"love mercy." And the question which immediately suggests itself is, Why should mercy be regarded as a distinctively religious requirement? Is it not an impulse of nature, always, everywhere? Can we say that the nations outside of Judaism were bereft of this quality? It is true that, measured by modern culture, they carried on war on a savage scale. But I have always felt that war is a bad test of the power of individual sympathy. On the field of battle men are not individuals, they are mechanical corporations, designed for a test of destructive power, but altogether free from personal animosity. It is true, also, that the Roman advocated in the most literal terms the survival of the fittest, and

would have arrested at the hour of birth the
life of defective forms.   And yet, deeply as
I deplore that such a phase of culture should
ever have existed, I am not prepared to say
that in every case it sprang from a hard
heart.   Rather do I think that in many in-
stances it came from a mistaken search for
mercy itself, and was dictated by a desire
to liberate these afflicted beings from the
necessity of meeting a world in whose
many mansions there was no place for
them.

But the emphatic word in Micah's creed
to my mind is not the word "mercy," but
the word "love"; and it is here, as I take
it, that both the originality and the religion
come in.   The old world certainly under-
stood the *quality* of mercy by the light of
human nature.   But I venture to think that
neither in the old world nor the new has
the *love* of mercy been generated apart from
the Christian principle; and I shall en-
deavor, very briefly and very succinctly, to

indicate the line of thought which has led me to this conclusion.

So far as known to me there are only four sources from which mercy can flow. Its origin may be either instinctive, philosophical, scientific, or humanitarian. The last is the distinctively Christian motive; and, on the result of its comparison with the other three, will be determined the question whether and to what extent the principle of Micah's creed is an evangelical principle. Let us glance in turn at each of these.

And first. There is an instinctive mercy in the heart of man. It is described by one word—pity. Pity is the instinct of mercy, and it belongs to man as man. But is pity also the *love* of mercy? Love supposes some object of attraction. Does pity imply an object of attraction? Is the sensation of pity one of attraction at all? In the living being attraction involves a certain amount of pleasure. Is not the sensation of pity one of pain? I think it is. It is true men go to witness on the stage scenes of horror. But they do not go on *account* of the horror; they wish to see the situations of dramatic power which the horror will bring forth. Pity is a sensation which in itself and by itself is painful, and therefore repulsive. The men of the most pitiful nature are precisely those who wish most to avoid it. Where will you find a kinder-hearted soul than Oliver Goldsmith? No beggar's cry could reach his ear without emptying his pocket. And yet, if Oliver saw the beggar in the distance, he turned the corner to escape him. It was not the wish to protect his money; it was the desire to escape the pain of a sad story. How many a young minister making his parochial rounds feels exactly the same in relation to the contact with sorrow! I speak under the influence of personal memory. I can remember in early days the self-congratulation I felt when I was privileged to witness

no scenes—when I had a day with no part-
ings, no bereavements, no cries for bread.
It would be all very noble if at such times
we imagined that we had escaped painful
scenes because there were none to be had.
But we know quite well that we have only
missed them because they have fallen into
the hands of another—because they lie on
the other side of the street. The instinct of
pity is a pain. We hold it in the heart
with tremor. We do not breathe freely
under its influence. We are oppressed by
the weight of its presence. We are re-
pelled from similar experiences. We
would fain avoid a second meeting. We
accept the sensation as an accident; we
struggle with it as Jacob struggled with
his angel. This, surely, is not the love of
mercy!

The second source of mercy is philosophy.
Its representative in this form is the Stoic.
The phase of mercy to which he has mainly
addressed himself is the forgiveness of in-

juries.   But the ground on which he com-
mends this is from our point of view suggestive.   He is impelled, not by the love of
mercy, but by the love of calm.   He deprecates anger, hatred, malice, and all unchar-
itableness ; but he does so because they disturb self-culture.   Anger is a pain, and the
philosopher should be superior to pain.   All
excess of emotion is weakness.   The blasts
of passion that sweep across the soul de-
prive it of its dignity and strip it of its
power.   The wise man should keep within
doors when the gusts are raging.   He should
refuse to yield to any solicitations of revenge.   Revenge is a wave upon the sea ;
it breaks the level of the waters.   The level
of the waters must not be broken.   Life
must be an equable calm, rising not, falling
not—a windless, waveless deep upon whose
surface there broods no storm.   The picture
of philosophic rest is incompatible with the
play of passions.

   It is true ; but it is incompatible with

more ; it is incompatible with the love of
mercy too. It is here that the contrast appears between the Stoic and the Christian.
The Stoic would conquer angry passion by
reducing the heart to stillness. The Christian would subdue it by inspiring the heart
with a new movement—a counter-passion,
the passion of love. The Stoic's mercy is a
negation—a holding back lest he should hold
the sword. The Christian's mercy is itself
a sword—what Paul calls the sword of the
Spirit. It is a weapon raised against anger,
a force which battles down the forces of
revenge. Christ's mercy breaks the calm
of the sea wherever it finds it. It cannot
tolerate indifference in a world of wrong.
It repudiates a peace where there should
be no peace. It advocates no insensibility
to injury. Rather would it make the sense
of injury a motive for healing the man who
has done it. "Lay not this sin to their
charge" is not a cry that comes from a
blunted sense of wrong. It is the voice of

one who is deeply conscious of having been injured, and who therefore is deeply concerned for the injurer. It is a mercy springing from a quickened, not a diminished, feeling of pain.

The third form of mercy is what I have called scientific. It is distinctively modern. It is affecting daily the decision of our criminal courts. It is built upon the notion that man is a piece of mechanism made to play a certain tune. If the mechanism is up to the mark the music will be good. If the mechanism is defective the music will be discordant. If the mechanism is hopelessly deranged the music will be non-existent, the man will be a criminal.

This is a view quite distinct from either instinctive pity or Stoic calm. It is founded upon the theory that man is a poor creature at best, and a very poor creature at worst. Indeed between the best and the worst there is no moral difference. It is a matter of physical organization. To visit crime with penalty is a metaphor, a legal fiction. It is a survival of the child's instinct to smash the door when it is angry. A man goes wrong as an organ goes wrong, as a watch goes wrong. Retribution, in any strict sense of the word, is out of the question. In the one case as much as in the other it is a disorder of the mechanism. A spring is broken, a chord is broken, a note is wanting, a string of the instrument has been relaxed. It is a matter for regret, but not for anger.

Now, I am not here discussing materialistic evolution, and with this theory in itself I have nothing to do. I am only concerned with its bearing on the creed of Micah. I do not ask whether it is false or true. I say, be it false or be it true, it is not the love of mercy. It is founded on contempt, on disparagement. Contempt cannot benefit its object. It can arrest retribution, but it cannot confer favor. It may commute the sentence, but it will not employ the offender after he has served his term. It will

readily consent to spare the men of Nine-
veh; but it will demur to send to them even
so poor a teacher as Jonah. The very
ground of its forgiveness paralyzes its
power to aid. It says, " This is a helpless
creature, and therefore not to be helped."
It pardons on account of incompetency;
on account of incompetency it also passes
by. It can refuse to *strike*, but it is nerveless to *redeem*.

In startling contrast to this is the fourth
and final mercy—that which I have called
humanitarian, which is popularly called
the mercy of Christ. It is founded upon
exactly the opposite basis—the *possibilities*
of man. It is built upon the belief that
man is not a mechanism but a soul. What
it sees is not the present state of dilapida-
tion ; it is the promise and potency of life.
All other streams of mercy have their source
in the aspect of the hour—instinct, philosophy, science. But the mercy of Christ has
its eye, not upon the man who is, but upon

the man who shall be. It sees, not the present, but the coming hour—not the cloud of to-day, but the possible sunshine of to-morrow. It looks, not *at* the rags and tatters, but *through* them. Through the patches of the rent garment it catches gleams —not of this year, but of next. It is the future which stimulates its arm. It imputes its own righteousness. It figures its object in the light of the morning. It considers what the organ would be if it had perfect stops, what the watch would be if it had adequate springs. Not because the man is a poor creature is it constrained to save. The constraint comes from the opposite perception—from the vision of his potential glory. The mercy of Christ is in the valley, but it is not *born* in the valley. It is born in the uplands—in hope. It endures the cross, not for the grief that confronts it, but for the joy that is set before it. It is the mercy of love, and therefore it works by faith—the sight of to-morrow.

The hand which impels it is the hand which is stretched through time "to catch the far-off interest of tears." The love of mercy is the mercy of love, and love has gladness mingled with its pain. The man who shall soar to this height in his own strength may pronounce the creed of Micah an easy thing.

" Walk Humbly With Thy God "

The way of the cross rightly borne, is the one way to the everlasting life. The path that threads the Garden of Gethsemane and climbs over the hill of Calvary, alone conducts to the visions of the Easter morning and the glories of the Ascension mount. If we will not drink of His cup, or be baptized with His baptism, or fill up that which is behind of His sufferings, we cannot expect to share in the joys of His espousals and the ecstasy of His triumph.—F. B. MEYER in " *Peace, Perfect Peace.*"

" Walk Humbly with Thy God "

WE have now arrived at the third article
of the creed of Micah. The first, justice,
relates to my actions as an *equal*. The
second, mercy, relates to my actions as a
superior. The third, humility, relates to my
actions as an inferior or dependent. Now,
in coming to this third, our first impression
is one of wonder. We are surprised that
Micah should have selected an act in which
the moral precept was so easy, " Walk
humbly with thy God." Why not "with
thy fellow-man"? Is it not in humility
with man that the difficulty of the precept
appears? What need to tell a poor trem-
bling human soul to be humble before God?
Are not the bravest awestruck there? Is it
possible for a frail and erring spirit to
realize the presence of God and not bend

the knee? We can understand very well how in the temple of nature a man may fail to *realize* God's presence. But if he has once come to *walk* with God, if he has once seen the King in His beauty, if he has once "tasted that the Lord is good," how can he do otherwise than bow? Is not the very vision of God the vision of contrast? If I believed Him to be my equal, He would be no longer a God to me. To walk humbly with God is a redundancy. I can walk humbly or proudly with my fellow-man; there is a choice of alternatives with *him*. But when I meet with God there is no alternative. If I walk at all I must walk looking up, with my eyes lifted toward the hills. Surely the prophet has been guilty of an anti-climax here!

Nay, but we have mistaken the meaning of the prophet. I, at least, believe that he means something very different. I hold that all through he is thinking of man, not God. I take him to have had in his mind the simile of a subject walking with his sovereign. The subject is naturally very proud of his company, proud of being seen in the companionship of one so much above himself. He is eager that men should see in what society he moves. He takes the most public streets, the most open thoroughfares. He lingers at the chief corners on the most trifling pretences. He is desirous that none of his friends or enemies shall by any chance miss the spectacle of that high favor which has been conferred upon him. It is not in the presence of his *sovereign* that he is proud; it is in the presence of his fellow-man. He is anxious that his neighbor should pass accidentally by, to see his social glory, to wonder, to envy, to say, "I wish I were in your place." He would like his brother to know that royalty has deigned to recognize him.

Now, let us apply this; we shall see that the pride which Micah deprecates is a pride before *man*. The Jew believed himself to

be walking with God, and to be walking
alone; he claimed a light which the surrounding nations had not. His attitude
toward the God with whom he walked
was deeply humble—I should say rather *too*
humble; he was afraid to commune with
Him. But though he was too tremulous to
enjoy his walk with God, he had a great
pride in the reputation of it. He wanted
the surrounding nations to look at him as
he passed by. He desired men to see that
he had a peculiar privilege, that he was a
marked man, a distinguished man. He
wished those on the world's road to be
aware that he was one out of the common
—chosen, precious. His walk with God
was not a *state* of pride, but it was a
source of pride. He boasted of it; he dis-
played it. On the ground of it he separated
himself from his kind. He dwelt apart
from the nations. He recognized haughtily
and at a distance the brotherhood of common men. He flourished in his hand that

torch which gave him superior illumination, and he bade the outside multitude attend and admire.

Such is the pride which Micah says pure religion must conquer. The question now is, What religion ? Is this an easy thing to subdue ? Is it conquerable by natural forces ? That has been tried—nothing has been so much tried. The great struggle of the old faiths was to find a panacea for pride. All asceticism, all sacrifice had its root there. Brahmanism was built upon the basis of self-humiliation ; Buddhism was reared upon the structure of self-extinction. The light of Asia was kindled at a sacrificial fire, and the motive of its kindling was the conquest of pride.

Has the old world succeeded ? Let us first ask what it has aimed to do. It awakened one morning to the sense that it was possessed of great beauty; and along with it there came the sense of great pride. It was distressed about its pride, and, to get rid of it, it resolved to slay the beauty. It did slay the beauty; did the pride die? On the contrary, it became proud of its beauty slain—of its own marred visage. It began to glory in a strength which had been powerful enough to pluck up so fair a flower. What was this but a new form of homage to the old thing? When I boast of any sacrifice I testify to the attraction of the object sacrificed. I tell my God, I tell myself, I tell my fellow-men, that it has still dominion over me.

The truth is, no man is entitled to get rid of his pride in this way—by the process of immolation. He is not entitled to get rid of it in any way which would involve the denial of a privilege. Humility is not the denial of a privilege. If I tell you you are beautiful, you are not bound in the interest of humility either to *say* that you are not or to *feel* that you are not. You are not of necessity a whit less humble though you should answer, "It is true; I know it; I have always known it." It is not in this direction that humility lies. I would go the length. of saying that if there is no sense of privilege there is no room for humility. The valley implies the height; where there is no height there can be no valley. To deny the existence of your mountain is not to be humble; to appreciate the existence of your mountain is not to be proud. To walk humbly with your God in the sight of men is to walk humbly with your strong point, your possession. Nature can teach a man to be docile in his weakness; it cannot tell him how to be humble in his strength. It can convince him that he is a poor creature; it cannot make him bend under the load of conscious riches. That is a humility which has come with Christianity alone.

What, then, is the power which enables a man to walk humbly with his strong point? It is love. The humility of Christ is reached, not by subtraction, but by addition; it is "more life and fuller" that we want. Let us say, You have come to the knowledge that you are possessed of a special revelation, a light which has not been given to other men. You are not entitled to undervalue that light. But, to prevent you from getting proud over it, there requires to be something added to your nature—the love of your brother man. What will be the effect of this love? It will cause you to say: Why should this beautiful light not be shared ? Must I keep so great a privilege to myself ? Ought not others to be partakers of this joy ? While I have it alone, it burns as well as brightens me. The detraction from its glory is the solitude in which I hold it.

This is the distinctively Christian humility; this is the humility of Christ. I used to wonder how Christ could call Himself humble—lowly in heart. It is vain to say that such riches as His could be unconscious of themselves; they neither could nor ought

to have been. Theologians have spoken
of "the full assurance of faith." They
mean that if a man has spiritual life he
ought to know it. Nay, why argue the
matter? There is nothing more certain
than Christ's knowledge of His own great-
ness, and it is never so certain as in that
very passage in which He declares His
heart to be lowly—His offer of universal
rest. Where, then, does the lowliness
come in? Why have I ceased to wonder
at the claim to humility on the part of
Jesus?

Because I have discovered that evangelical humility is the opposite of unevangelical.
The humility of nature says, "I have nothing; I am a poor creature." It is a very easy
thing to say, easier still to feel. The spectacle of death itself would teach it. But
the humility of the Gospel says: "I have
something; I am not poor. I feel the presence of a gift within me. That gift makes
me a debtor. I dare not hoard it. I may

not keep it to myself. If I had nothing I might be ministered unto; but because I have a gift I must be a servant. My possession is my call to what men name humiliation. I am bound to work, because I have an inheritance. I am the servant of every man who has not my privilege. I can have no rest until I have shared it."

That is the humility which Christianity imputes to her Lord. "Father, I will that these whom Thou hast given Me be with Me where I am, that they may behold My glory." It is from the full sense of possession that He speaks. He is gazing on a scene of glory; but around Him are a multitude of the blind. He cannot bear the solitary sight—the thought that others have it not. The brightness scorches Him; the undivided joy is piercing pain. He longs to let others see. He would rather not look at it in the presence of the blind; His privilege is sore upon Him; He veils His face from the glory. That is the lowliness of

Jesus, that is the lowliness of Christian souls. It is the pain of possession, the burden of having a gift alone. It is the demand that my fullness should share itself, my goodness should give, my love should serve. It is the ministration of master minds, the helpfulness of holy hearts, the need that the highest natures should take the lowest room. Those whom Christ calls the poor in spirit are they who have already received the kingdom.

www.ingramcontent.com/pod-product-compliance
Lightning Source LLC
Chambersburg PA
CBHW031817090426
42739CB00008B/1305